York leads you through secret alleyways and the city's own 'Diagon Alley' – the iconic Shambles.

These walks encounter various people who, over the centuries, have made York the city we know today. From the Roman Emperor Constantine to George Hudson the 'Railway King', the city has been home to figures as diverse as Guy Fawkes, highwayman Dick Turpin, writer Kate Atkinson and chocolate tycoon Joseph Rowntree.

Among the city's secrets are dozens of life-like cat sculptures, perched above cafés and shop windows. Architect Tom Adams kick-started York's cat craze in the 1980s when he commissioned sculptor Jonathan Newdick to add cats to the buildings he designed. Six of the walks have hidden cats to discover, and even a mouse. Can you spot them all?

The Village Walks section visits sights outside the city centre: ancient meadows, reed-fringed streams, chocolate factories and pioneering architecture. And there's more to discover further afield in the glorious Yorkshire countryside: from castles to the coastline, heather-covered moorland and rolling wooded hills.

Whether you love history, architecture or books, or are Harry Potter's biggest fan, a chocoholic, or just love taking a city stroll with some good pubs along the way, around every corner York has a story to tell.

ABOVE A view from the city walls, overlooking Grays Court Hotel Garden with majestic York Minster in the background.

CITY WALKS

WALK THE WALLS

Miles of masonry and a millennia of history
make a perfect introduction for visitors

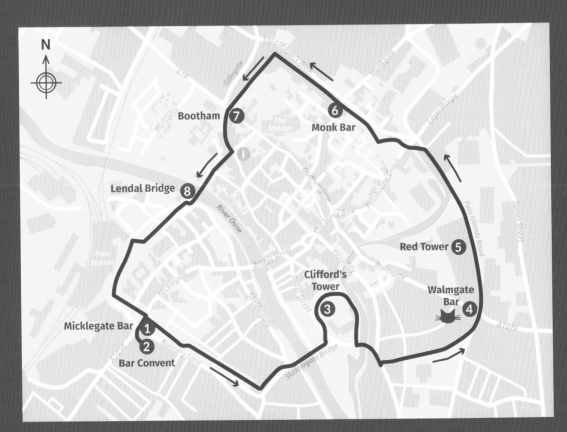

York's medieval walls, England's longest
surviving example, stand on the line of earlier
fortifications dating back to the Romans.
From high on the walls, there are views of the
Minster and other ancient buildings, which are
explored in the walks that follow.

 SPOT THE CAT

Look towards a ledge outside the lower
window of the café at Walmgate Bar

Cross the road outside the railway station and turn left. At the junction, keep straight over the road towards the statue of George Leeman (see page 15) and turn immediately right through the arch. Climb the steps onto the walls and walk back past the station. Continue round the corner ahead, to **Micklegate Bar ❶**, chief of York's four main medieval 'bars' (or gateways) where the severed heads of traitors once topped the walls. It's now home to the Henry VII Experience, the first Tudor king. Take a detour down onto Blossom Street to visit the **Bar Convent ❷**, England's oldest active convent; it has a heritage museum and a café in the walled garden.

Go on around the city walls and, eventually, down steps onto Skeldergate. Turn right to the main road, left over the River Ouse, and left on Tower Street to visit **Clifford's Tower ❸**, the remains of York Castle. The views from the top stretch as far as the North York Moors. Return to Tower Street, follow the road over the River Foss, cross Piccadilly, and climb back onto the wall through the arch ahead.

The next big gate is **Walmgate Bar ❹**, which has a café inside the tower. Go on along the walls and, at the end, turn right around the brick-built **Red Tower ❺**. The next section was once a huge swamp so there was no need for a defensive wall. Turn left along busy Foss Islands Road, soon walking beside the River Foss. Cross over Peasholme Green to re-join the wall.

Follow the walkway again to arrive at **Monk Bar ❻**, complete with medieval toilet and portcullis. Head down the steps onto Goodramgate and look for a little doorway beside the arch to take you back up to the top floor of the gatehouse, passing the Richard III Experience.

Go on, past views of York Minster and across lovely gardens, round a final corner to reach **Bootham ❼**, where the walkway goes through the room above the archway and then ends. Through the floor of the Croque-Monsieur café, built into the gate, you can glimpse the Roman defences underneath the medieval walls.

Keep ahead at the foot of the steps, past the Theatre Royal, towards the Visit York Information Centre. This is the starting point for the next walk, which explores Roman York, including the ruins in the nearby Museum Gardens. Turn right along Museum Street and cross **Lendal Bridge ❽** to return to the station.

ABOVE York's city walls date back to 71 AD and stretch over 2 miles (3.2 km). Around 2.5 million people walk the walls every year.

BELOW The bottom half of Micklegate Bar dates back to the 12th century. The top storey was added in the 14th century to accommodate a portcullis and a barbican.

BOTTOM Clifford's Tower, the remains of York Castle, dates back to the 13th century. It has been used as a treasury and a prison.

CITY WALKS

START: **Visit York Information Centre, Museum Street**
END: **Roman Bath pub, St Sampsons Square**
DISTANCE: **One mile / 1½ kilometres (plus museums)**

ROMAN YORK

Discover York's Roman past, the birth
of the city we know today

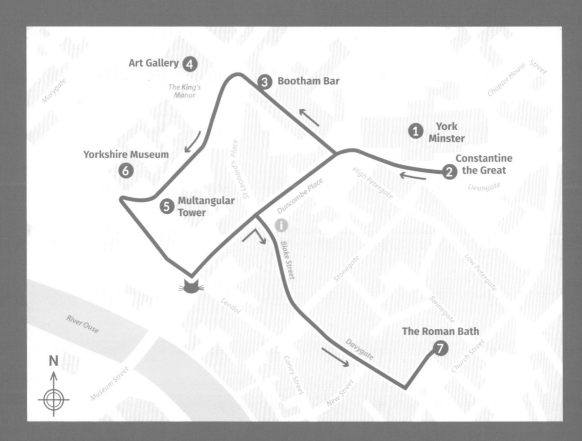

Five thousand Roman soldiers marched into
what is now York in 71 AD and founded
Eboracum, the largest fortress in northern
England. They remained for 300 years.
This walk explores what they left behind.

 SPOT THE CAT

As you leave Museum Gardens, glance
up at the building right of the junction
across the road to find a black cat
outside a first floor window

From Visit York Information Centre, walk down Duncombe Place towards **York Minster ❶**, built over part of the Roman fortress. Turn right in front of the Minster, to find a modern bronze statue of **Constantine the Great ❷** nearby. In 305 AD, the Emperor Constantius died in Eboracum and the Roman soldiers there declared his son Constantine their leader. Emperor Constantine united the Roman Empire and promoted Christianity. The neighbouring Roman Column gives a sense of the impressive scale of Eboracum.

Enter the Minster and head down to the Undercroft to see the ruins of a Roman basilica. Go back to the front of the minster and keep straight along High Petergate, which was the Roman main street (*via principalis*), to **Bootham Bar ❸**. This is one of York's four medieval city gates and stands on the site of a main entrance into the Roman fortress.

On the far side is the **Art Gallery ❹**. Upstairs, a seventeen-metre wall of pots represents York's history in ceramics – from Romans to the present day. Take the tarmac path next to the King's Manor and follow it into the museum gardens, dotted with stone sarcophagi (Roman coffins). To the left, you will find the **Multangular Tower ❺**, York's best-preserved Roman ruin and only remaining tower from the original fortress. Look out for the decorative band of terracotta in the Roman lower half.

The **Yorkshire Museum ❻**, in a nearby neoclassical building, has one of the best collections of Roman objects in Britain, including a mosaic floor and fresco found in York and a statue of Mars, the Roman god of war. Bones and belongings from six different Roman citizens show how cosmopolitan Eboracum must have been. Turn left out of the museum, through the gates ahead, and left onto Museum Street to return to Visit York.

REFRESHMENTS The Roman Bath ❼
For a drink with a Roman theme, turn right at Visit York into Blake Street and follow it into Davygate. At St Sampson's Square, turn left for the Roman Bath. There are remains of the soldiers' communal bath house in a small, atmospheric museum under this pub.

BELOW The bronze statue of Constantine the Great outside York Minster was unveiled in 1998.

CONSTANTINE THE GREAT
A.D. 274 – 337
PROCLAIMED ROMAN EMPEROR
IN YORK A.D. 306

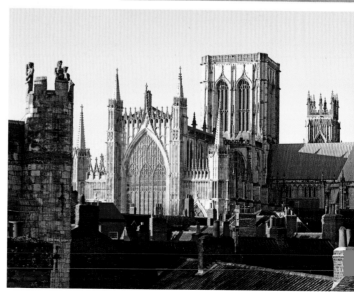

RIGHT York Minster with Bootham Bar to the left.

START: **Museum Gardens**
END: **Jorvik Viking Centre, Coppergate**
DISTANCE: **1½ miles / 2½ kilometres**

VIKING YORK

Come face to face with Viking warrior king Olaf,
and visit the recreated world of Jorvik

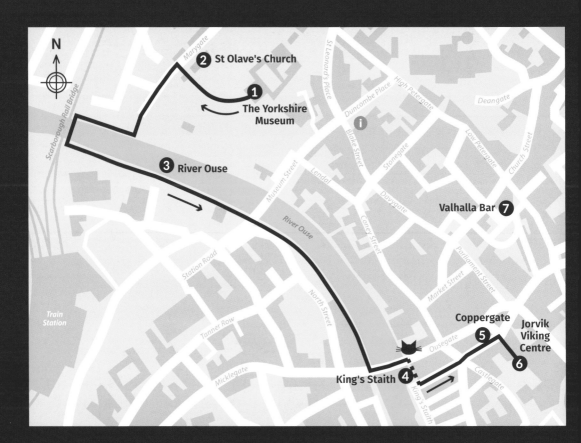

Ever wondered why so many of York's street names end in 'gate'? It comes from *gata*, the Viking word for street; York has lots of place names recalling its Scandinavian heritage. In 866 AD, Ivar The Boneless and his Vikings arrived in York and Saxon Eoforwic became Jorvik – capital of a Viking kingdom.

 **SPOT THE CAT**

Immediately after crossing the river again, look up at the walls and windows above Amplifon and STA Travel

The Yorkshire Museum ❶ has some evocative Viking exhibits downstairs, like a leather boot found in Coney Street and a twisted gold ring from Hungate. Walk past the ruins of St Mary's Abbey and leave the gardens through the gate on the far side into Marygate.

On the right **St Olave's Church** ❷ was first dedicated in 1055 to the Norwegian Saint Olaf, a Viking warrior king. Earlier that century, Olaf's army attacked London Bridge by boat and may have inspired the song 'London Bridge is Falling Down'. The statue above the church door is Olaf as a warrior. Go into the church and look at the stained glass window behind the altar to see Olaf crowned as a more peaceful king.

Turn left outside the church along Marygate and turn right at the river. Cross Scarborough Rail Bridge and turn left on the far side of the Ouse. Walk along the waterside path, through the stone arches and under Lendal Bridge, keeping straight on the road and riverside walkway beyond. The Vikings arrived in longboats on the **River Ouse** ❸ and the river gave the Vikings access to the North Sea coast, via the Humber, meaning York could trade with the continent. During this time, York had pots from Germany, amber from the Baltic, and silks from China. Walk along the river to the next bridge and cross back over.

Turn right along **King's Staith** ❹, a cobbled quay beside the often-flooded Kings Arms pub. *Staith* is another Old Norse word, meaning a 'wharf' or 'landing place'. Turn left up King Street and over Nessgate into Coppergate, from a Viking word for carpenters.

Archaeologists dug up **Coppergate** ❺ when the shopping centre was built and found lots of Viking relics. Turn right at Caffè Nero to find out more at the **Jorvik Viking Centre** ❻. This popular ride-through attraction recreates the sights, sounds (and smells!) of 8th-century Britain with animatronic Viking fishermen, huntsmen and blacksmiths. Six metres under the city streets, you can see the actual remains of a Viking fire-pit and share the excitement of discovering buried Jorvik, the once-bustling Viking town.

REFRESHMENTS Valhalla Bar ❼
This Viking-inspired pub on Patrick Pool boasts signature dishes that are named after Norse gods. The award-winning Odin's Judgement Ale comes from the Yorkshire Heart brewery just outside York.

ABOVE Statue of Olaf as a warrior king above the door of St Olave's Church.

ABOVE The picturesque River Ouse, the gateway for the Viking army back in 866 AD.

CITY WALKS

LITERARY YORK

Every corner tells a story

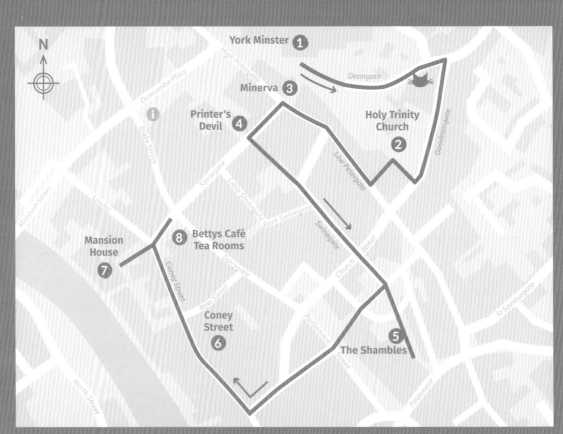

Storytelling has a long tradition in York. The city's cobbled lanes and ancient buildings have inspired centuries of writing, from medieval religious playwrights to JK Rowling. A serpentine walk winds through some of York's fairytale alleyways, which will appeal to story lovers old and young.

 SPOT THE CAT

Just after turning right into Goodramgate, look above the window of the Goji café

Charles Dickens and the Brontë sisters visited **York Minster** ❶. Dickens stayed at the Black Swan inn (see page 12) while he was researching cruel Yorkshire boarding schools like the one in *Nicholas Nickleby*. The novel also includes a story based on the Minster's Five Sisters stained glass window. In 2000, York Minster was one of the venues for a huge revival of the medieval Mystery Plays. The plays were traditionally acted on waggons in the city streets and tell the Christian story from Creation to the Last Judgement. They still take place in York every four years.

Outside the Minster, head left past the Roman Column into Deangate and right into Goodramgate. Just after the Happy Valley restaurant (in one of York's oldest houses), turn right through a gateway to visit the candlelit **Holy Trinity church** ❷ – take the next right if it's shut. A rainbow-bordered plaque celebrates diarist Anne Lister, who married her lover Ann Walker in this church in 1834. The BBC drama *Gentleman Jack* is based on Lister's diaries.

Turn left down the narrow alleyway from the church and right onto Low Petergate. At the junction with Minster Gates (once known as Bookbinders' Alley), look up to see a statue of **Minerva** ❸, Roman goddess of wisdom, with a pile of books. Turn left here onto Stonegate, once renowned for printing presses and bookshops. Opposite the Evil Eye bar, turn left into Coffee Yard, through an archway decorated with a red **Printer's Devil** ❹, a symbol from when hot type was carried by boys known as 'devils'.

Walk on, past 14th-century Barley Hall and keep straight along Swinegate and Patrick Pool, towards the **Shambles** ❺. This picturesque medieval street – York's most famous thoroughfare – has a gruesome story. It used to be full of butchers' shops and

ABOVE York Minster is one of the England's most iconic buildings, and northern Europe's biggest Gothic cathedral. This architectural masterpiece took 250 years to build and receives over 2 million visitors each year.

BELOW The Printer's Devil, also known as the Stonegate Devil and the Little Red Devil.

ABOVE Minerva, the Roman goddess of wisdom.

ABOVE The Shambles, York's most famous street, and the city's own 'Diagon Alley'. INSET The film set of Diagon Alley in the Warner Bros. Studio Tour London.

the name 'shambles' came from an early word for slaughterhouse. The runnels in the road allowed blood to flow away. This mysterious street inspired the set for Diagon Alley, the fictional shopping lane where students from Hogwarts buy their school equipment in the Harry Potter films. Narrow, cobbled and crowded with quirky cafés, it's easy to imagine Ollivander's wand shop or the Leaky Cauldron pub tucked in among them and several shops at the far end have Potter-related themes. Halfway along the Shambles, look out on the right for the Shrine of Margaret Clitherow, a little oasis of calm among the camera-clutching tourists. Saint Margaret Clitherow hid Catholic priests in this house and was executed in 1586 – pressed to death on Ouse Bridge.

Return to Newgate, turn left along Jubbergate and keep straight across Parliament Street into Market Street. Continue and turn right at the end into **Coney Street** ⑥. Look out for the faces and devils above TK Maxx. In 1849 Charlotte and Anne Brontë stayed at the George Inn, which was where Next is

now. The Church of St Martin Le Grand, with its ornate clock, has a stained glass window with scenes from St Martin's life.

Daniel Defoe's character of Robinson Crusoe was born in York and appears in a stained glass window in the riverside Guildhall, behind **Mansion House** ⑦ residence of York's Lord Mayor. The Mansion House, recently re-opened after a grand refurbishment, is full of interesting artefacts, from the huge Georgian pies in the basement kitchen to the silver collections on the second floor. Stroll through St Helen's Square to find the famous **Bettys Café Tea Rooms** ⑧ on the right.

REFRESHMENTS **Bettys Café Tea Rooms**
Detective Jackson Brodie has coffee here in Kate Atkinson's novel *Started Early, Took My Dog*. Atkinson was born in York and her prize-winning first novel *Behind the Scenes at the Museum* is set in the city.

CITY WALKS

HAUNTED PUB CRAWL

Dare you explore the ghostly corners
of Europe's most haunted city?

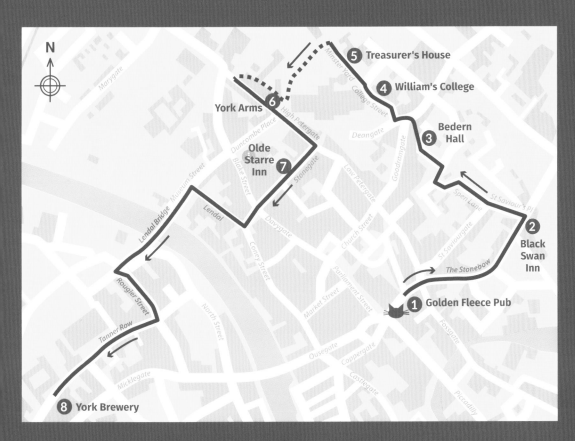

N

5 Treasurer's House
4 William's College
York Arms 6
Bedern Hall 3
Olde Starre Inn 7
2 Black Swan Inn
1 Golden Fleece Pub
8 York Brewery

York is said to have as many inns as days of the year and this crawl links pubs with ancient halls through a labyrinth of cobbled alleys and narrow streets and passages, known as snickelways. Representing various styles and centuries, these buildings all have one thing in common: ghosts!

 SPOT THE CAT

A spectral feline can be seen emerging from the wall of the Golden Fleece at the start of the walk

ABOVE With its gruesome history, and lined with wonky buildings that resemble haunted houses, it is no surprise that the Shambles is York's oldest and spookiest street.

Start outside the **Golden Fleece ❶**, York's most ghost-infested pub, with wonky walls, four-poster beds and fifteen different resident spectres, including Lady Alice Peckett, who wanders the corridors and moves the furniture in the night. The nearby Shambles is also brilliantly spooky at night and a favourite haunt for ghost tours.

Turn right out of the pub, passing St Crux Church, where a police officer reported hearing funereal music late one night. Walk along The Stonebow to the **Black Swan Inn ❷**, in Peasholme Green. An upstairs room has old wood panelling and a tiled fireplace and there are several resident ghosts. They include a bowler-hatted gent, who waits impatiently at the bar before fading away; a large black cat, and a spectral highwayman nicknamed Jack, who appears in the kitchen in boots and long black cloak. Historical highwayman Dick Turpin was imprisoned in York Castle and is buried nearby.

Cross the road outside the pub and follow St Saviour's Place and Spen Lane. Keep straight along a little path to St Andrewgate, past the church, and continue along Bartle Garth ahead. Follow this lane right past **Bedern Hall ❸**, where an evil 19th-century schoolmaster killed orphan children and

kept them in cupboards. They are said to haunt the area, with invisible hands and disembodied shadows.

Turn left, past an old chapel and through an arch onto Goodramgate. Turn left and immediately right around the half-timbered National Trust gift shop into College Street. Follow the lane past **St William's College ❹**, troubled by the ghost of a thief who killed a priest and then his own brother, for fear he would confess, and finally, remorsefully, himself.

Continue into Minster Yard, where the **Treasurer's House ❺** has had ghostly Roman legionaries marching through the cellar, visible only from the knees upwards – the old Roman road is buried eighteen inches under the cellar floor. Harry Martindale, who saw them in 1953, observed unexpected details (like green tunics and round shields) that were only verified by later archaeological finds. Turn left through Dean's Park (when the gates are locked walk the other way round the Minster).

Turn right out of the gates into Precentors' Court, left through the tiny passageway at the end and left again on High Petergate to the **York Arms ❻**, haunted by a nun once bricked up in a wall here. Continue along High Petergate, past an inn named

ABOVE Owned by the National Trust, Treasurer's House, particularly its cellar, is home to some of the city's most famous ghost sightings.

for Guy Fawkes, conspirator in the famous 1605 Gunpowder Plot to kill King James; Fawkes was born nearby in 1570 and went to school in York. Bar staff at the Guy Fawkes, which has a suit of armour (nicknamed Jimbob) in its dark-panelled, dim-lit parlour, have encountered rocking chairs that move by themselves and other invisible forces.

Turn right into Stonegate, where York's most ancient hostelry, the **Olde Starre Inn** ⓻, at number 40, is one of many spooky inns. Black cats used to be bricked up alive inside walls, believing they would bring luck, and customers have heard mysterious scratchings near the bar. Civil war casualties were treated in the Olde Starre, where ghostly screams occasionally rise from the cellar and an old lady has been seen climbing the stairs. A grey lady has also been seen many times in York's Theatre Royal, round the corner. Continue to the end of the road; turn right onto Lendal, and left over the bridge.

Go on along Station Road, turn left into Rougier Street, passing lots of pubs, and right along Tanner Row to reach the **York Brewery** ⓼, where you can try the award-winning Centurion's Ghost Ale at source and even take a tour. The brewery has a maze of rooms dating back to the 18th century and used to be a morgue so it's no surprise to hear tell of mysterious footsteps, self-moving tables and a tall, thin, top-hatted spectre, who slams the doors. Drink up!

ABOVE The grotesques and gargoyles that decorate the exterior of York Minster protect the cathedral from evil spirits.

START AND END: **York Railway Station**
DISTANCE: **1 mile / 1½ kilometres**
TRANSPORT: **You can also arrive by road train from Duncombe Place, near York Minster**

TRAINSPOTTING IN YORK

From steam trains to bullet trains, this walk will keep you 'on track' in York's transport hub

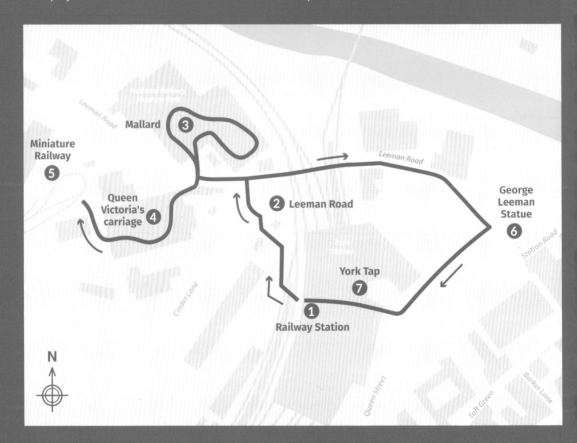

If you're fanatical about trains, you're in the right city! From Stephenson's rocket to Japanese bullet trains, model railways to classic station architecture, you can see it all. Halfway between Edinburgh and London, it's not surprising that York's railway station is an important transport hub. Next door, the world's largest rail museum spans three centuries of railway history.

DID YOU KNOW?

No steam locomotive since has beaten the 126 mph record set by *Mallard* in 1938

Start inside the magnificent **Railway Station** ❶ and look up. In his 2017 book *Britain's 100 Best Railway Stations*, Simon Jenkins gave York a five star rating and praised the 'grandeur of its roof': glazed and supported on classical columns, with Corinthian capitals. Look out for wrought iron white roses of York (see Contents page) and the old wooden signal box, which is now a café.

Climb the steps behind this signal-box-café, passing a spectacular clock and walk along the raised bridge over the platforms to emerge behind the station. Go down the steps and follow the fenced path. Just before **Leeman Road** ❷, turn sharp left into the National Railway Museum. The road is named after George Leeman, politician, lawyer, and chair of the UK's Railway Association, who helped create the North Eastern Railway Company in 1854.

Go inside the museum and turn right, down and up steps and past the Countess of York carriage-tearoom, to the Great Hall. Walk right to find the **Mallard** ❸, the world's fastest ever steam train. Nearby is a Eurostar engine and an early Japanese bullet train. Go on into the North Shed to learn about the Flying Scotsman and explore the museum's labyrinthine collections.

This includes a marble bust of George Hudson. Nicknamed The Railway King, he was responsible for York becoming a major rail hub and was – for a while – a national hero. He invested in the North Midland Railway Company and eventually managed more than one thousand miles of track. Hudson's business methods were controversial and the scandal when his funds ran out eventually ruined him. Nevertheless York still owes him its railway legacy and there is a George Hudson Street close by.

Go back past the main entrance into the Station Hall to see **Queen Victoria's carriage** ❹ – an ornate 'palace on wheels'. Head out into the South Yard to enjoy steam train rides and a **miniature railway** ❺. Return to Leeman Road, and turn right through a pedestrian tunnel under the railway. Go on past the Post Office depot and follow the road right. On the left-hand side of the stone arch ahead, you can see York's first public statue: **George Leeman** ❻, carved by York sculptor George Walker Milburn in 1885, stands above the traffic on Station Road.

TOP The iconic roof of York Railway Station, with the famous clock at the top of the steps.

ABOVE Queen Victoria's personal train in the National Railway Museum.

Turn right, past the yellow brick Principal, built as the Royal Station Hotel in 1878. Head back to the station for a drink at the **York Tap** ❼; the North Eastern Railway built this art nouveau building in 1907 as the tearoom.

LOOK OUT FOR Harry Potter fans will find many familiar sights on this walk: a station clock and footbridge like those Harry and Hagrid pass at King's Cross; old-fashioned train compartments like the ones on the Hogwarts Express (in Station Hall) and a sign saying Platform 9¾ (in the museum's collections).

YORK'S SWEET STORY

Take this mouth-watering jaunt and
discover the Chocolate City

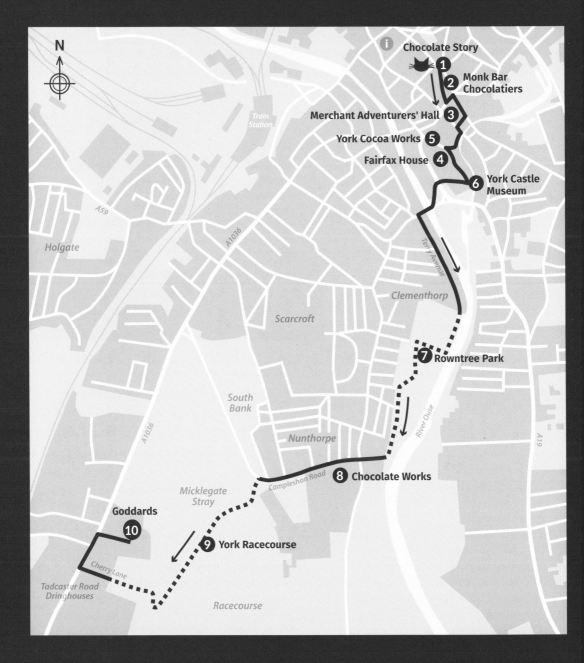

N

1 Chocolate Story
2 Monk Bar Chocolatiers
3 Merchant Adventurers' Hall
5 York Cocoa Works
4 Fairfax House
6 York Castle Museum
7 Rowntree Park
8 Chocolate Works
9 York Racecourse
10 Goddards

Holgate
Train Station
A59
A1036
Scarcroft
Clementhorp
Terry Avenue
South Bank
A1036
Nunthorpe
River Ouse
A19
Micklegate Stray
Campleshon Road
Goddards
Cherry Lane
Tadcaster Road Dringhouses
Racecourse

VILLAGE WALKS

Some northern cities are built on steel or wool, but York is built on chocolate. Terry's Chocolate Orange, Smarties and other world famous brands were all invented in York. Tributes to the pioneers, the Rowntree and Terry families, are seen throughout the city. This walk meanders along the river and across York racecourse to the former village of Dringhouses.

ABOVE The Merchant Adventurers' Hall, one of the finest examples of a medieval guildhall in the world, and home to the Company of Merchant Adventurers of the City of York.

 SPOT THE CAT

Next to the Chocolate Story, search the roof of the Duke of York pub to find a cat stalking a pigeon. Look out too, as you go along the Shambles, for cats above York Glass Works and the Edinburgh Woollen Mill.

AND THE MOUSE

Yorkshire-based designer Robert Thompson carved choir stalls for York Minster and other local churches. He also made the altar rail for St Edward's church near Goddards and left his signature motif – a little mouse – carved into the wood.

Turn right outside York's **Chocolate Story ❶**, an interactive museum with lots of opportunities to taste. From a cup of unsweetened chocolate with chilli to go with the epic introductory video, to a make-your-own chocolate lollipop, there's something to try in almost every room. They also have their own chocolatier, whipping up yummy fresh fillings, such as mango and cardamom.

Take a turn through the Shambles Market with stalls selling handmade fudge or tray-baked cake bars and then stroll along the picturesque Shambles, past **Monk Bar Chocolatiers ❷**, one of York's many artisanal chocolate shops.

Turn left along Pavement (the first Rowntree store was to the right, where Pizza Hut is now) and right onto Fossgate

ABOVE Rowntree Park pond, with the Reading Café in the background.

to visit the **Merchant Adventurers' Hall** ❸ through an archway next to the Hairy Fig delicatessen. This is said to be one of the finest examples of a medieval guildhall in Europe. The Company of Merchant Adventurers controlled York's trade for centuries and still own this fine, beamed hall with a great garden café.

Make your way past the hall, up steps onto Piccadilly and turn left. Turn right before the bridge onto a path beside the River Foss. Turn right into Coppergate shopping centre and left at Carluccio's, past Scoops ice cream kiosk, to find **Fairfax House** ❹. This elegant Georgian townhouse recreates the grandeur of eighteenth century York with furniture from the Terry family home.

To the right on Castlegate, on the far side of Fairfax House, is the **York Cocoa Works** ❺. This new chocolate academy, shop and café is taking forward the city's luscious legacy on the site of a warehouse that once belonged to Mary Tuke, the independent Quaker woman who started the business that became Rowntrees of York. Walk back along Castlegate and keep straight past Clifford's Tower to the **York Castle Museum** ❻. Kirkgate, a reconstructed street full of Victorian shop fronts includes a real sweet shop and a Cocoa Room.

Cross Tower Street below Clifford's Tower and walk diagonally left through the riverside gardens. Cross Skeldergate Bridge and turn left along Terry Avenue beside the water to reach pretty **Rowntree Park** ❼. Joseph Rowntree gave this park to the City of York in 1921 as a memorial to cocoa workers killed in World War I. Turn right through the main gate towards the pond and café, left along the lake and out through the avenue and gates beyond.

Keep right and, soon after passing the Millennium Bridge to your left, turn right by a green dog bin along a hedged path. Keep straight along Reginald Grove into Campleshon Road past the new **Chocolate Works** estate ❽. Look left across the grass to see the distinctive brick clock tower of what was once the Terry's factory, opened in 1926, which produced the famous Chocolate Orange.

At the end of Campleshon Road, walk straight and slightly right, through a gate ahead, onto **York Racecourse** ❾. Continue over the race track itself (on race days, you'll need to go round by road). Turn right and immediately left across the field, following a long grassy path between white fences, leading diagonally across the racecourse. Exit through a small car park on the far side and keep straight onto Cherry Lane.

Turn right along Tadcaster Road, Dringhouses, past the church, to find **Goddards** ❿. This lovely Arts and Crafts house was once home of the Terry family and has a confectionary-themed exhibition upstairs. Catch any of the frequent buses back into town from near the Cross Keys pub over the road.

REFRESHMENTS
Rowntree Park and Goddards have cafés with outdoor terraces, where you can have lunch or fresh home-made cakes. Help yourself to sherry in the drawing room at Goddards (donations in the pot).

BELOW Now owned by the National Trust and a popular Arts and Crafts house, Goddards was the home of the chocolate-making Terry family.

START: **Haxby Village (bus from York Art Gallery)**
END: **York Art Gallery**
DISTANCE: **6 miles / 10 kilometres**
TRANSPORT: **Bus number 1 runs to Haxby from outside York Art Gallery every 12 minutes**

ALONG THE RIVER FOSS

Take a break away from the hustle and bustle of the city with this riverside stroll

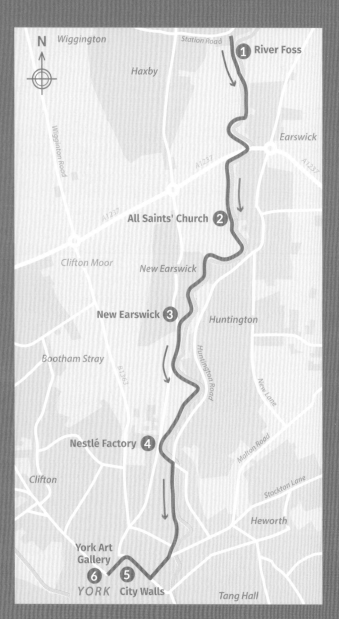

There are more sweet surprises on this peaceful meander from the town of Haxby back into York. The walk combines urban and rural: a waft of cocoa from the Nestlé factory and the flash of a turquoise kingfisher; York's medieval city walls and its hidden green corridors.

Start by catching bus number 1 from outside York's Art Gallery to Haxby, about twenty minutes out of town. At the end of the walk, you can choose to follow the city walls back to the gallery or keep straight along the Foss and round the southern walls towards York Castle. Not far beyond that, the Foss flows into the River Ouse near a picturesque blue footbridge.

FUN FACT

Joseph Rowntree built the brick houses of New Earswick in 1902 for workers in his chocolate factory

LEFT A peaceful stroll along the River Foss provides views of buildings old and new, celebrating York's past and present.

BELOW Not only was Joseph Rowntree one of the most important chocolatiers in Britain, he was also a famous philantropist and advocate of social reform.

Leave the bus at Haxby's Memorial Hall and walk along Station Road, keeping straight past the mini-roundabout. Turn right at the footpath sign into Landing Lane. At a post with waymarks, turn left onto a path beside the **River Foss** ❶.

Cross a footbridge and continue on the far side of the river. At the next footbridge, cross back over and follow the riverbank, with the river on your left again. Keep straight past **All Saints' Church** ❷, turn left onto the lane beyond and right before the brick bridge at a sign for Willowbank. Follow the river over stiles through peaceful fields.

Passing the garden village of **New Earswick** ❸, you can detour right along Station Avenue to a café in

the Folk Hall for a delicious slice of cake and coffee. Continue along the riverside path, joining the Haxby Road for about 200 metres, and turning left at a footpath sign, back to the riverside. Watch out for water birds and the smell of chocolate from the **Nestlé Factory** ❹. Reaching a bridge ahead, climb the steps and cross the road. A riverside path continues, but for a greener route, turn right on the road, left onto Fossway, over the bridge, and right through the gates into a park.

As you reach the bridge at Heworth Green, turn right to the roundabout and left to follow the pavement with the river on your left. Keep going until you see the **City Walls** ❺ ahead. Turn right and walk along the walls back to **York Art Gallery** ❻.

START AND END: **Heslington Hall**
DISTANCE: **2½ miles / 4 kilometres**
TRANSPORT: **Bus 66 goes there every fifteen minutes from outside the railway station**

UNIVERSITY OF YORK

Merging ancient meadows and iconic modern architecture, walk through a thousand years of history

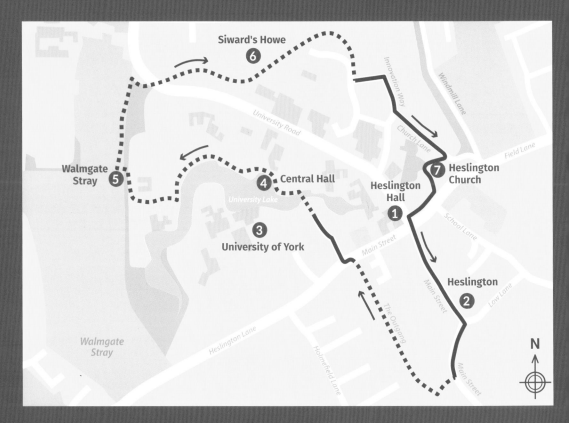

York's university surrounds Tudor Heslington Hall and stretches past picturesque lakes to Walmgate Stray, one of York's remaining areas of common land. Behind Heslington Hall is a lovely, peaceful garden, with a pond, summerhouse and topiary box hedges, known as The Quiet Place. Many of the other buildings are pioneering examples of 20th-century architecture.

DON'T MISS

York University's Central Hall, built in the 1960s, looks like a spaceship that has landed on the water

ABOVE Heslington Hall is a Grade II listed manor house. Today it is part of the campus of the University of York.

Cross University Road from the bus stop to take a look at **Heslington Hall ❶**. First built as a country house in 1568, this manor is now an integral part of the University of York. Return to University Road and take a right turn along Main Street into the village of **Heslington ❷**, passing pretty brick houses. Turn right at the end and follow the road as it curves left past fields. Turn right, opposite Lowfield House along a lane called The Outgang. Turn right from a car park along a gravel track and left before No. 1 along a path. Follow the path right between trees, with houses on your left. Keep straight past allotments, along a wooded path and finally take the lane back to University Road.

Cross over, turn left along the brick wall and right into a walled lane. Follow this tarmac path into the **University of York ❸**. Turn right before the private sign and keep straight over a footbridge ahead. Turn left beside the water past the modernist **Central Hall ❹**, part of the university's 1960s expansion. Keep going, with the water on your left, to reach the gleaming new Environment Building, opened in 2016. Turn right before this building. Keep straight on the road ahead and follow it along the edge of the campus.

Turn left at a blue sign towards Fulford into **Walmgate Stray ❺**. York's green 'strays' are ancient fields around the city; to explore them more, follow the city council's Millenium Way (booklets are available from Visit York). Turn immediately right along a path through trees and follow it uphill to the tarmac lane. Turn right and immediately left through a tunnel under the main road. Follow the cycle path ahead, passing the site of an Anglo Saxon burial mound near the big water tower on **Siward's Howe ❻** or Heslington Hill. Siward was a Danish warrior, mentioned in Shakespeare's *Macbeth*. He died in York in 1055.

Keep following the cycle path. Turn left at the junction towards Tang Hall and then right into the Science Park towards the futuristic tower ahead. Turn left on Church Lane towards the spire of **Heslington Church ❼**, a Victorian parish church with Arts and Crafts features. Turn right at the noticeboard, into the churchyard, and right across the grass beyond, back to Heslington Hall.

REFRESHMENTS
Visitors can use the university's canteens, like the waterside Edge café, and there are two pubs in Heslington.

VILLAGE WALKS

START AND END: **Castle Howard's stable block (next to car park and bus stop)**
DISTANCE: **5 miles / 8 kilometres**
TRANSPORT: **Bus 181 from York to Malton via Castle Howard leaves every
couple of hours from Station Avenue and entitles you to a discounted
entrance ticket**

CASTLE HOWARD

Explore one of England's finest stately homes

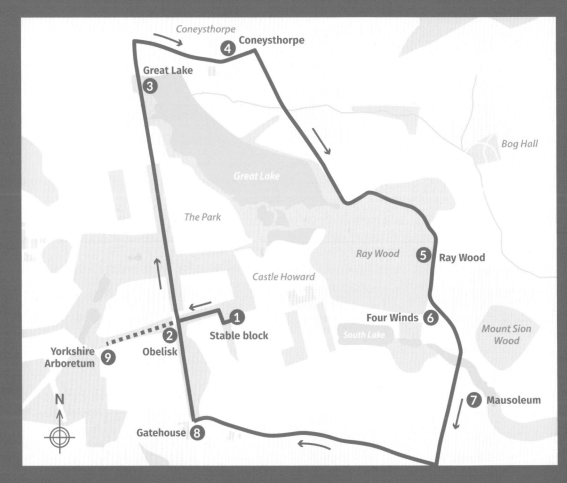

Surrounded by the rolling Howardian Hills, Castle Howard has grand interiors and formal gardens to enjoy. Still a private home to the Howard family, it is a beautiful example of English baroque architecture, with miles of landscaped lawns, lakes, groves and temples.

FUN FACT

Castle Howard became Brideshead Castle for both the 1981 TV serial and the 2008 film of *Brideshead Revisited*

Walk along public paths through woods and on country lanes, and pass through some lovely corners of the estate that many visitors will miss.

Turn right out of Castle Howard's **stable block** ❶, which has been converted into a farm shop, and left at the white sentry post to the **Obelisk** ❷. Turn right along the wide grassy verge of the road, past ponds and bridges, and a glimpse of the **Great Lake** ❸.

Just after the gateposts and lodge house, turn right onto a lane. Keep straight past Lakeside Holiday Park and the pretty village green at **Coneysthorpe** ❹. Soon after houses end, turn right through a white-painted gate onto a path signed Welburn.

Keep straight on a stony track and follow it left. Turn right onto another path signed Welburn, winding through the trees. Turn right onto a track at the end and continue through a white gate and along the wall of **Ray Wood** ❺.

At the Temple of the **Four Winds** ❻, head diagonally left across the grass to a three-arched bridge and cross over. From the bridge, there are fine views of the domed **Mausoleum** ❼. Designed by the architect Nicholas Hawksmoor in 1729, the magnificence of this tomb prompted Horace Walpole to say it was a building that might 'tempt one to be buried alive'.

Keep straight on a track ahead and turn right at the junction onto a tarmac lane, passing a pyramid on your left. Stay on this lane to emerge near a spectacular **Gatehouse** ❽. Turn right along the road to return to the Obelisk. The left turn off this roundabout leads, in a few hundred metres, to the **Yorkshire Arboretum** ❾.

REFRESHMENTS
Lovely cafés at Castle Howard and at the Arboretum are open to the public with or without entrance tickets to the Castle itself.

BELOW The impressive south aspect of Castle Howard with the Atlas fountain in front.

LONG DISTANCE PATHS

York is the perfect base for some of
the country's top scenic trails

From strolls in the rolling wolds, to longer coastal and moorland
hikes, the countryside beyond York offers spectacular walking
opportunities. National Trails are long-distance paths through
Britain's wildest and most beautiful landscapes. Two National
Trails – the Cleveland Way and the Yorkshire Wolds Way –
run not far from York. Even closer to the city, there are routes
that explore river valleys or ruined castles, history and nature.

ABOVE Views from the Cleveland Way, a 110-mile hike that combines both coastline and moorland.

One of the UK's most spectacular trails, the 110-mile Cleveland Way starts in the pretty market town of Helmsley, with its ruined castle and walled gardens, an hour's drive north of York (31X bus from the Art Gallery). The opening miles take travellers near **Rievaulx Abbey** 1 in the green Rye valley and you can loop back to Helmsley via the neoclassical temples on the National Trust's Rievaulx Terrace – perfect for picnics! The Cleveland Way goes on, over rocky, heather-covered moors, to the Yorkshire Coast, where it ends at Filey, an hour's drive east of York (trains back via Seamer).

The seaside town of **Filey** 2 is also one end of the 80-mile Yorkshire Wolds Way, which has its own share of breath-taking scenery. Starting near the **Humber Bridge** 3, an hour's drive south-east (trains via Brough), the trail winds through gentle wooded hills and chalky valleys, with views that stretch out for

miles. It passes the deserted medieval village of **Wharram Percy** 4, ancient churches, flowering fields and cliff-top works of art.

The Centenary Way, devised to celebrate 100 years of North Yorkshire County Council, joins the Wolds Way through the hills to Filey. It starts from York Minster and heads out of town along the River Foss (see page 20), looping through the rolling landscapes around **Castle Howard** 5. The Foss Walk and the Ebor Way also run alongside the River Foss. The 70-mile Ebor Way, which takes its name from the Roman name for York, passes right through the city on its way from Helmsley to **Ilkley** 6.

Another great area for walking is the varied countryside around **Fountains Abbey** 7, 45 minutes drive from York. The National Trust offers a choice of routes, from an hour or so strolling by the lake to an eight-mile hike from Ripon past the deer park and Georgian water garden.

Other routes that pass through York itself include the **Wilberforce Way**, a 60-mile trail that celebrates the abolition of slavery in 1807. William Wilberforce, MP for Yorkshire at that time, campaigned against the slave trade: the route starts in **Hull 8**, where he was born, and ends at York Minster. On the way, the path goes through Heslington and the University of York (see page 22).

York's city council recently devised the 23-mile **Millennium Way** though nearby fields and urban villages; it passes the Millennium Bridge and the racecourse (see page 19) as well as ancient meadows like Walmgate Stray (page 23). With trains and buses connecting the ancient city with extraordinary countryside, York has even more to offer beyond its busy streets and age-old monuments.

BELOW The breathtaking ruins of this 12th-century Cistercian abbey show it to have been one of the finest examples of monastic architecture in Europe. Fountains Abbey, and the surrounding area, has been designated a UNESCO World Heritage Site.

OPPOSITE Colourful huts at Scarborough's sandy North Bay beach.

BELOW A sign for the 80-mile Yorkshire Wolds Way. The trail runs from the Humber estuary to the headland of Filey Brigg.

YORKSHIRE COAST

If you do like to be beside the seaside, head for Scarborough and experience the wild cliffs and golden sandy beaches

FUN FACT

Between Whitby and York, the Coastliner bus stops at Goathland steam railway station, which became Hogsmeade Station in the first Harry Potter film, *Harry Potter and the Philosopher's Stone*

The Cleveland Way boasts twenty miles of cliff-top walking between Scarborough and Whitby. Packed with classic coastal views and picturesque villages like Robin Hood's Bay, it is perfect for a weekend walk. You can reach them both on the Coastliner bus from York, and Scarborough is also less than an hour by train.

Seaside **Scarborough** ❾, is a castle-topped town just made for strolling: wrought-iron bridges, gardens full of winding, wooded pathways, and promenades with views of the sparkling sea. The Stephen Joseph Theatre, where Alan Ayckbourn's plays still premiere, is just opposite the station and the Art Gallery is a five-minute walk.

You can make your way through the gardens behind the gallery or take the nearby cliff tramway down to the donkey-trampled beach. Turning left along the sand, you reach the harbour, and – beyond that - the hilly maze of paths that wind around rocky Scarborough Castle (great place for a picnic). On the far side of the hill, near the castle entrance, is St Mary's church, where Anne Brontë is buried.

Heading back to the station, you pass the covered market and the Assembly Rooms, where Charles Dickens gave a reading.

Whitby ❿, famous for fish and chips, jet, and a ruined abbey that inspired Bram Stoker's Dracula, is another iconic seaside destination. The scenic X93 bus runs between Scarborough and Whitby every half an hour, through forests, fields and open moorland, so you can walk as much or as little as you like of the coast path between them, or hop on the bus.

From Whitby harbour, climb the 199 steps up to the spiky Gothic abbey and follow the Cleveland Way along the cliffs. You could turn right after two miles at the lighthouse and follow the lane back to the abbey. Turn left by St Mary's church along Aelfleda Terrace to go back down to the harbour via Caedmon's Trod, a gentler, more peaceful route than the popular 199 steps.

The ride over the moors from Whitby back to York on the 840 Coastliner bus is one of England's wildest, with wide, heather-purple views.

BELOW Catch the stunning sunrise over North Bay in Scarborough, with The Grand Hotel in the town centre and the Castle just visible on the cliff top.

PLACES TO VISIT

Admission fee unless marked *free*.

Art Gallery
Open daily 10–5
01904 687687
www.yorkartgallery.org.uk

Bar Convent
Open Mon–Sat 10–4
01904 643238
www.bar-convent.org.uk

Barley Hall
Open 10–4
01904 615505
www.barleyhall.co.uk

Bettys Café Tea Rooms
Open daily 9–9
01904 659142
www.bettys.co.uk

Castle Howard
Gardens open daily 10–5
01653 648333
www.castlehoward.co.uk

Chocolate Story
Open for tours daily 10–4
01904 527765
www.yorkschocolatestory.com

Church of St Martin, Coney Street *free*
01904 636512
www.stmartinsyork.org.uk

City Walls Walk *free*
www.yorkwalls.org.uk

Clifford's Tower
01904 646940
www.english-heritage.org.uk/ visit/places/cliffords-tower-york

Cocoa Works
Open daily
01904 675787
www.yorkcocoahouse.co.uk

Fairfax House
Open 10–5 Tues to Sat, 11–4 Sun
01904 655543
www.fairfaxhouse.co.uk

Fountains Abbey
Open daily 10–6
www.nationaltrust.org.uk/ fountains-abbey-and-studley- royal-water-garden

Goddards
Open daily 10.30–4
01904 771930
www.nationaltrust.org.uk/ goddards

Helmsley Castle
Open daily 10–5
01439 770422
www.english-heritage.org.uk/ visit/places/helmsley-castle

Henry VII Experience
Open 10–3
01904 615505
www.henryviiexperience.co.uk

Holy Trinity Church *free*
Open Mon–Sat, 11–3.30
www.visitchurches.org.uk/visit/ church-listing/holy-trinity-york

Jorvik Viking Centre
Open 10–4
01904 615505
www.jorvikvikingcentre.co.uk

Mansion House
Open Wed–Sun 10.30–4.30
01904 553663
www.mansionhouseyork.com

Merchant Adventurers' Hall
Open Sun–Fri 10–4
01904 654818
www.merchantshallyork.org

National Railway Museum *free*
Open daily 10–5
03330 161010
www.railwaymuseum.org.uk

Richard III Experience
Open daily 10–4
01904 615505
www.richardiiiexperience.com

Rievaulx Abbey
Open 10–5
01439 798228
*www.english-heritage.org.uk/
visit/places/rievaulx-abbey*

Roman Bath
Open 11–4
01904 620455

Rowntree Park *free*
Open 8am–dusk

Shrine of Margaret Clitherow
free
Open daily
01904 624767
*www.stwilfridsyork.org.
uk/shrine-st-margaret-
clitherow.php*

St Olave's Church *free*
Open daily
www.stolave.org.uk

Theatre Royal
01904 623568
www.yorktheatreroyal.co.uk

Treasurer's House
Open 11–4
01904 624247
*www.nationaltrust.org.uk/
treasurers-house-york*

University of York *free*
01904 320000
www.york.ac.uk

Valhalla Bar
01904 653999
www.valhallayork.com

Wharram Percy *free*
*www.english-heritage.org.uk/
visit/places/wharram-percy-
deserted-medieval-village*

York Brewery
Opening times vary
01904 621162
www.york-brewery.co.uk

York Castle Museum
Open 9.30–5
01904 687687
www.yorkcastlemuseum.org.uk

York Minster
Open from 9am, Mon–Sat
01904 557200
www.yorkminster.org

York Racecourse
*free to walk across on
non-race days*
www.yorkracecourse.co.uk

Yorkshire Aboretum
Open 10–4 Feb–Nov
01653 648598
www.yorkshirearboretum.org

Yorkshire Museum
Open 10–5
01904 687687
www.yorkshiremuseum.org.uk

RIGHT The Shambles: York's oldest and most famous street.

Written by Phoebe Taplin
Edited by Sophie Nickelson

Photography © AnitaImage

with the exception of:
Alamy Stock Photo: 10 (inset), 15 (bottom), 21, 28 (bottom), 29, 30
Phoebe Taplin: contents (inset), 7 (left), 18, 19, 23, 25, 27, 28 (top)
Visit York Information Centre: 5 (bottom)

ISBN: 978-1-84165-837-7

1/19

Printed in Turkey

Pitkin Publishing
Pavilion Books Ltd
43 Great Ormond Street
London WC1N 3HZ

+44 (0)20 7462 1500

www.pavilionbooks.com

Visit York

Special thanks to Visit York for their contribution and support.
For more information please visit:
www.visityork.org